GLOBE FEARON

LITERATURE

LANGUAGE ENRICHMENT WORKBOOK

• Green Level •

GLOBE FEARON

Pearson Learning Group

Supervising Editors: Karen McCollum and Rosely Himmelstein
Editor: Ayanna Taylor
Editorial Developer: Pearson Education Development Group
Production Editor: Travis Bailey
Designer: Angel Weyant
Manufacturing Supervisor: Mark Cirillo

ISBN 0-130-23571-7
Printed in the United States of America

2 3 4 5 6 7 8 9 10 04 03 02

1-800-321-3106
www.pearsonlearning.com

CONTENTS

THE BET

Look at the pictures below. Identify the setting by telling the time and place of each one. Think about these questions to help figure out the setting. Are the pictures of long ago, the present, or the future? Where are the pictures from? What is it like there?

1.
TIME: _______________________________

____

PLACE: _______________________________

____

GENERAL
ENVIRONMENT: _______________________________

____

2.
TIME: _______________________________

____

PLACE: _______________________________

____

GENERAL
ENVIRONMENT: _______________________________

____

3.
TIME: _______________________________

____

PLACE: _______________________________

____

GENERAL
ENVIRONMENT: _______________________________

____

THE BET

A. Write sentences using the past tense of the verbs below. Each sentence should tell how the character in "The Bet" spent his time while he was imprisoned.

1. study ____

____

2. write ____

____

3. read ____

____

4. play ____

____

5. talk ____

____

6. cry ____

____

B. Close your eyes and visualize the lawyer's prison. On a separate sheet of paper, draw a diagram to explain your interpretation of the setting. Be sure to include what things his environment must have provided him with. Label the objects in your drawing.

C. Describe where and how the prisoner spent his time. Where did he spend the most time? What did he do there? What did he think about? If you like, you can work with a classmate.

____

____

____

____

____

THE BET

A. The words below are vocabulary from the story "The Bet." Arrange them in alphabetical order by numbering them 1 through 12. The first one is given.

_____ fretfully		_____ incarceration
_____ stake		_____ grope
_____ zealously		_____ ruble
_____ haphazardly		_____ theology
_____ volition		_____ philosophy
_1_ capital		_____ classic

B. Use a dictionary to review the meanings of words listed above. Then use them to complete the following sentences. Cross each word out as you use it.

1. It was obvious that the secretary had left in a rush because the work table was cluttered and papers were thrown _______________ over her desk.

2. Screaming and yelling, the football team _______________ celebrated their Super Bowl victory.

3. We could tell the telephone call had disturbed him because he grabbed his briefcase and _______________ ran for the elevator.

4. Entering the darkened theatre, the movie goers had to _______________ for their seats.

5. Every state has a city that is the center of its government, so it is called the state _______________ .

6. It was of his own _______________ that the lawyer made up his mind to stay in prison for fifteen years.

C. Write six sentences of your own, using the six words that you did not use from the list above.

1. ____

2. ____

3. ____

4. ____

5. ____

6. ____

LATHER AND NOTHING ELSE

In "Lather and Nothing Else," the narrator faces a problem that he must work through in his head. Think about a concern or problem that exists in your life. It may be a career or college choice, or trying to resolve a problem with a friend or family member.

1. Describe your concern or problem.

    ____

    ____

    ____

2. List in order the outcomes you wish would happen.

    ____

    ____

    ____

3. Tell the possible obstacles to the outcome(s) above.

    ____

    ____

    ____

4. Describe an action you could take to overcome an obstacle you listed.

    ____

    ____

    ____

5. What is the very best thing that could happen? Explain why you think so.

    ____

    ____

    ____

6. What is the very worst thing that could happen? Explain why you think so.

    ____

    ____

    ____

Name _______________________________   Date _______________________

LATHER AND NOTHING ELSE

A. Unscramble the words in the left column below. Notice that each word in the right column is a synonym (has the same meaning) of one of the scrambled words. Draw a line from the word in the left column to its synonym in the right column.

1. rida _______________   question

2. saveh _______________   cut

3. clsie _______________   hurt

4. oundw _______________   attack

5. botud _______________   scrape

B. Write two sentences for each unscrambled word listed above. In one sentence, use the word as a noun. In the second sentence, use the word as a verb.

1. (noun) ____

____

(verb) ____

____

2. (noun) ____

____

(verb) ____

____

3. (noun) ____

____

(verb) ____

____

4. (noun) ____

____

(verb) ____

____

5. (noun) ____

____

(verb) ____

____

ECCLESIASTES 3:1–8

A. Read the definitions given in the chart below. Choose a word from the Word List that fits each definition. Write it next to the definition. Next, find an antonym for the word you chose. Write it in the appropriate place. An example is completed for you.

Word List

praise	insignificant	vice	different
ruthlessness	obese	insult	graceful
bequeath	cowardice	compassion	courage
clumsy	inherit	important	slight
virtue	blunt	uniform	guilty

DEFINITION	WORD	ANTONYM
to express approval	praise	insult
cruelty; without pity		
right action; goodness		
unchanging; alike		
overweight; stout		
meaning a lot		
excessive fear		
awkward; without skill		
give property to another		

B. Choose two pairs of words from your completed chart above. For each word pair, write two related sentences. Use one of the words in each sentence.

Example: Everyone likes to receive praise.
               No one likes an insult.

1. ____

____

2. ____

____

ECCLESIASTES 3:1–8

Illustrate a comic strip based on the poem "Ecclesiastes 3:1–8." Follow these simple directions to help you complete your comic strip.

1. Choose three or four lines from the poem and write them in the space provided.

   ____

   ____

   ____

   ____

2. Think about what symbols, events, or actions can represent the activities that are expressed in the lines you choose. Write your ideas for each line.

   ____

   ____

   ____

   ____

3. Draw your comic strip with the ideas you have written. Use one box below to illustrate each line. Now, cover the top half of your worksheet and see if a classmate can guess which lines you have illustrated from the poem.

4. Which symbol(s) or events or actions did your classmate understand right away? Why do you think so? Which symbol or cartoon was hardest to understand? Why? ___________________________________

   ____

THE OATH OF ATHENIAN YOUTH

1. You are a bystander at a demonstration about a controversial social issue. Describe what you see.

____

____

____

____

____

2. Now describe the demonstration from a different point of view. You are a person involved in the demonstration. Write what you observe.

____

____

____

____

____

____

____

3. Was one point of view easier to describe than the other? Why or why not?

____

4. What is the point of view used in "The Oath of Athenian Youth"? How is it similar to the first point of view you used? Would another point of view be possible for "The Oath of Athenian Youth"?

____

____

____

____

THE NECKLACE

A. Read the statements in the chart below. Put an X beneath the name of the character who fits the information. Statements may suit one or all of the characters. The first one is completed for you as an example.

STATEMENT	LOISEL	MATHILDE	JEANNE
1. loved only the fine things in life		X	
2. suggested that a jewel be borrowed			
3. looked for bargains, insulted shopkeepers			
4. paid the jeweler 36,000 francs			
5. first noticed the necklace was gone			
6. young and beautiful at the story's end			
7. went to search for the lost necklace			
8. sacrificed 400 francs			
9. lived in France			
10. used inheritance to help pay debts			
11. lent the "glass" jewel			
12. felt the necklace should have been returned sooner			

B. Use your choices in the chart above to help you write a brief description of each character in "The Necklace."

Loisel ____

____

Mathilde ____

____

Jeanne ____

____

THE NECKLACE

A. Bring characters to life by helping to create them. Fill in the blanks in the story to develop the characters. You can use as many words in the blanks as you want. Now, on a separate sheet of paper, draw a picture of Becky and the woman to illustrate the story you wrote.

Becky was a(n) ______________ who enjoyed ______________ . She liked

to wear ______________ and ______________ . She had ______________

hair, ______________ eyes, and a(n) ______________ nose. One afternoon

______________ , Becky noticed a ______________ . She quickly

______________ and ______________ . As she did this she thought

______________ . At the same time, a ______________ woman who wore a

______________ and had ______________ hair passed by and thought

______________ . Then she said, "______________ ." Becky replied,

"______________ ."

B. From your completed passage and drawings write a brief description of Becky's and the other woman's appearance and personality.

Becky ____

____

____

____

____

other woman ____

____

____

____

____

THE SHEPHERD-BOY AND THE WOLF/ THE BUILDERS

The **theme** of a literary work is the underlying meaning the author wants
to relate to the reader. "The Shepherd-Boy and the Wolf" and "The
Builders" are poems derived from fables with definite themes.

Answer the following questions about theme.

1. a. What is the underlying theme of "The Shepherd-Boy and the Wolf"?

    ____

    ____

    b. Which line in the poem best expresses the theme?

    ____

    c. In "The Shepherd-Boy and the Wolf" the boy "cries wolf." What has the term
        "cries wolf" come to mean?

    ____

2. a. What is the underlying theme of "The Builders"?

    ____

    ____

    b. In which lines can you find the theme?

    ____

    ____

    ____

    ____

POLAR NIGHT

Study the picture below.

1. What is the theme of the picture?

   ____

   ____

   ____

2. If you were asked to participate in the event taking place in the picture, would you? Why or why not?

   ____

   ____

   ____

   ____

   ____

3. What else could you do if you chose not to participate in the demonstration but still wanted to show your support for animal rights?

   ____

   ____

   ____

4. Write a slogan about animal rights that expresses a particular theme.

   ____

   ____

5. What animals today are endangered? Name at least three. What can be done now that could help the three animals you have listed to survive? Write your suggestions for each one.

   Animal A: ____________ . _______________________________

   ____

   Animal B: ____________ . _______________________________

   ____

   Animal C: ____________ . _______________________________

   ____

Name _________________________ **Date** _________________

TO NOEL/FEAR

A. In "Fear," Gabriela Mistral describes a mother's fears about losing her daughter. In the space provided, write three things that you are afraid might happen.

1. ____

2. ____

3. ____

B. Now, choose one of the three fears you have listed above. What could you use to represent your fears? List three things that could be symbols for your fears.

1. ____

2. ____

3. ____

C. Pick two symbols you have listed above. Explain the meaning of each symbol.

1. ____

____

2. ____

____

D. The narrator of "To Noel" describes a child's wish about gifts at Christmas. Think of something you have wished for very much. Write a paragraph to describe your wish. What does it mean to you? Why was it the most important thing in the world to you at the time?

____

____

____

____

____

____

____

____

____

THE SCARLET IBIS

A. In "The Scarlet Ibis," the ibis is used as an *extended metaphor*, or symbol, for Doodle. Describe the comparisons that are made in the story between Doodle and the ibis.

____

____

____

____

____

____

B. Think of a person who has been or is very important in your life. What animal or object do you see as a symbol for that person? In a paragraph of your own, explain why you chose that symbol.

____

____

____

____

____

____

____

____

____

____

____

____

Name _______________________   Date _______________

THE MONKEY'S PAW

A. Read the following sentences. Identify which element of the play *The Monkey's Paw* **each sentence describes. Use** *S* **for setting,** *P* **for plot,** *C* **for character, and** *T* **for theme. The first one has been done for you.**

_____S_____   **1.** It is a dark, rainy, cold winter's night.

___________   **2.** A sixty-year-old man, Mr. White, and his son, Herbert, play chess.

___________   **3.** The story is about a monkey's paw that has magic powers and can grant wishes, but the results are tragic.

___________   **4.** Mrs. White is a gray-haired woman who wants to buy new furniture.

___________   **5.** The living room and dining room are made warm by a fire.

___________   **6.** The wishes do not have the results that the Whites expected.

___________   **7.** A person's best intentions might bring unwelcome results.

___________   **8.** It is the English countryside in the 19th century.

___________   **9.** Mr. White makes a third and final wish.

___________   **10.** Sergeant-Major Morris is tall and red-faced.

B. Use the sentences you identified above to fill in the lines below. Use note form. Two examples are completed for you.

Characters:

Mr. White and Herbert play chess

____

____

____

Plot:

____

____

____

Setting:

dark, rainy, cold winter night

____

____

____

Theme:

____

____

____

THE PIT AND THE PENDULUM

(This activity includes pages 16–17.)

In "The Pit and the Pendulum," suspense is created by the terror and agony expressed by the narrator. The narrator tries to calm his fear by studying his cell, making calculations, and struggling for freedom.

A. Below are listed some situations that are suspenseful and/or fearful. Rank them in order from the one that is the most fearful to the one that is the least fearful to you. Use numbers 1–6, 1 being the most fearful and 6 being the least fearful.

_______________ a ferocious dog

_______________ a burglar

_______________ a battlefield

_______________ a violent thunderstorm

_______________ an auto accident

_______________ a swarm of bees

B. Think about the situation that you ranked as most fearful. On the lines below, explain why that situation makes you afraid.

____

____

____

____

____

____

____

____

____

____

____

____

THE PIT AND THE PENDULUM

(Continued from page 16.)

In the previous lesson you were asked to rank situations that may be suspenseful and/or fearful. Now, think about each situation and list possible solutions for handling the situation. Use complete sentences to tell what you would do in each instance.

1. a ferocious dog ____

____

____

2. a burglar ____

____

____

3. a battlefield ____

____

____

4. a violent thunderstorm ____

____

____

5. an auto accident ____

____

____

6. a swarm of bees ____

____

____

THE PIT AND THE PENDULUM

When you use a dictionary to find a word that is new to you, you will
see its pronunciation next to it. A symbol is used for each sound.

A. **Below is a list of some common pronunciation symbols, followed by a word with
the same sound. Add the letters given in parenthesis to either the beginning or
end of each word to form your own word that has the same sound. The first one is
completed as an example.**

1.	/a/	at	_____flat_____ (fl)
2.	/ā/	pain	_____________ (s)
3.	/i/	it	_____________ (spl)
4.	/k/	cat	_____________ (ch)
5.	/e/	bet	_____________ (ter)
6.	/ē/	eat	_____________ (m)
7.	/u/	fun	_____________ (ny)
8.	/z/	chose	_____________ (n)
9.	/ī/	rival	_____________ (ar)
10.	/ī/	sty	_____________ (le)
11.	/o/	off	_____________ (ice)
12.	/ō/	oat	_____________ (fl)
13.	/ū/	use	_____________ (am)
14.	/ə/	second	_____________ (ary)
15.	/sh/	shad	_____________ (ow)

**B. Now, look back at the exercise you have just completed. Say each word and circle
the letter or letters in the words you wrote that represent the sound shown by the
symbol. Then use three of the words in sentences.**

____

____

____

____

Name _________________________________   **Date** _________________

THE HITCHHIKER

Below are ten words taken from the selection "The Hitchhiker." Study the words. Then read the sentences below to decide which word best fits into each sentence. Use context clues to help you figure out the correct answer.

Word List

machine	license	piano	bonfire	amateur
highway	bargain	genius	profession	shoelace

_______________ **1.** The bright glowing light near the schoolyard let us know, even miles away, that the _______________ was burning fiercely.

_______________ **2.** Because Freddy's IQ was so high, we all believed that he was a _______________ .

_______________ **3.** My father wanted to buy a new red car, but the salesperson offered such a good _______________ on the blue truck that my father couldn't refuse it.

_______________ **4.** Sherry could not understand why she kept tripping over her shoes until she saw that her _______________ was untied.

_______________ **5.** During the boxing match, it was clear that the bigger fighter was an _______________ because his smaller opponent kept knocking him down with great ease.

_______________ **6.** Some of the buttons on my shirt fell off, so I was convinced that the _______________ used to sew them on was not working properly.

_______________ **7.** Stan's mother is a nurse. His father is a teacher. Even though both are proud of what they do, they have always encouraged Stan to choose whatever _______________ he is interested in.

_______________ **8.** Winding curves forced us to be extremely careful as we travelled on the _______________ .

_______________ **9.** Bobby was aware of the law that says in order to drive a car, one must first have a driver's _______________ .

_______________ **10.** Denise was so good at playing _______________ that people came from miles around to hear her in concert.

from KON-TIKI

Using the words in the box, label the drawing to show the parts of a sailboat. If some words are unfamiliar to you, consult a dictionary.

Word List

boom	rudder	bow	mast	forestay
starboard	stern	sail	port	deck

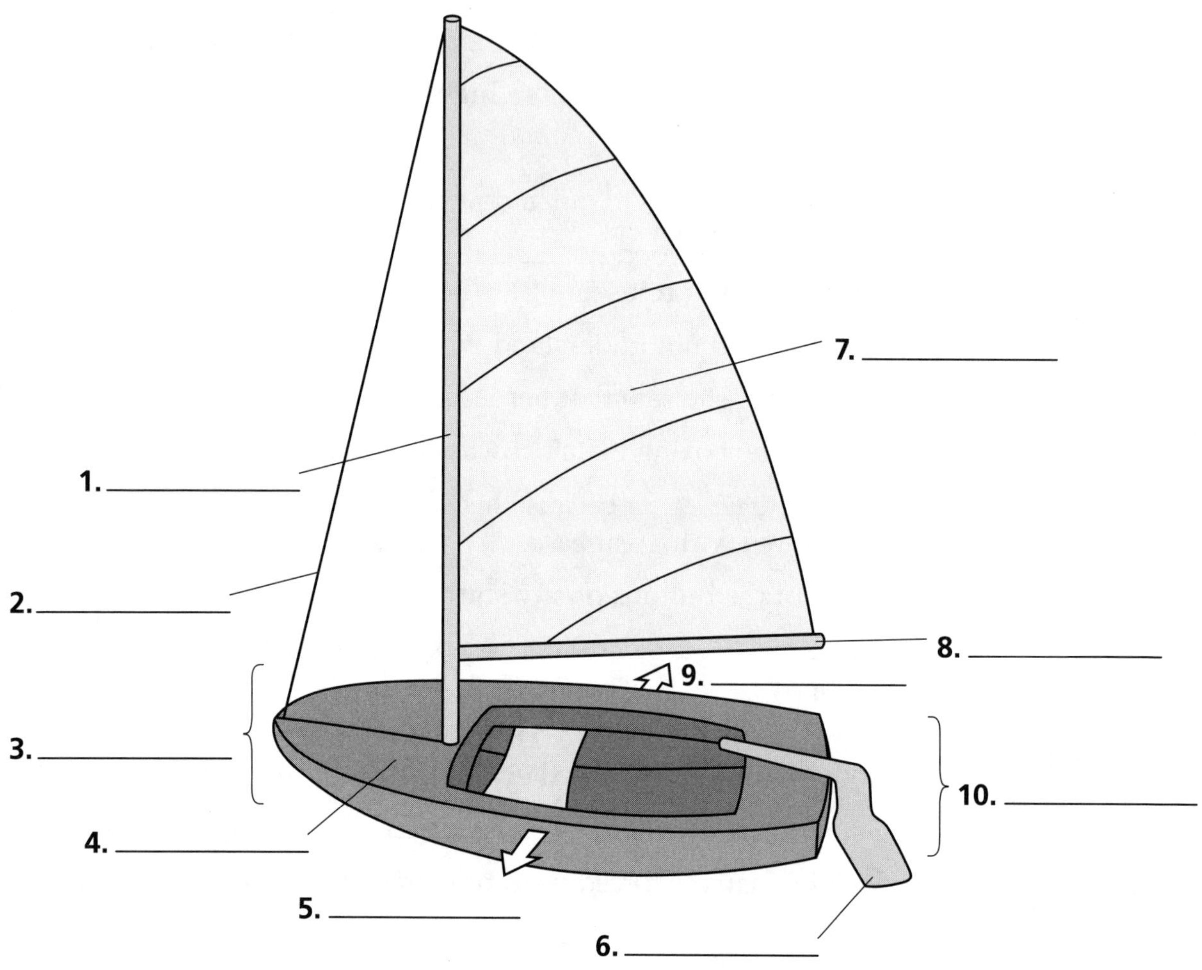

AUGUST HEAT

A. Below are descriptions of two characters in "August Heat." Take a moment to remember everything you can about each character. Then, put the letter that stands for that character next to the statements that tell about him. The first one is done for you.

A. James Withencroft

B. Charles Atkinson

1. _A_ in perfect health

2. _____ purple and scarlet flowers in his yard

3. _____ made tombstones

4. _____ was an artist

5. _____ said it was "hot as the devil"

6. _____ had a lapse of memory

7. _____ the narrator of the story

8. _____ had a red silk handerkerchief

9. _____ said the heat could make a man crazy

10. _____ was familiar with tools, especially chisels

B. Circle the statements above that tell about Charles Atkinson. Read them carefully. Decide if they help you make a prediction about what he will do. Use complete sentences and write down your ideas.

____

____

____

____

C. The words on the tombstone said "In the midst of life we are in death." What does this mean? Write what you think. Then discuss your idea with a classmate.

____

____

THE INTERLOPERS

Write the meanings for the italicized words in the sentences below. Use the chart of Latin roots and prefixes and any clues given by the rest of the sentence. After you finish, check your accuracy by finding the words' meanings in a dictionary.

ROOT PREFIX	MEANING	ROOT PREFIX	MEANING	ROOT PREFIX	MEANING
audi	to hear	terr	earth	aqua	water
bene	good, well	uni	one	ques	to ask, seek
ceed	to go	vac	empty	tempor	time
fer	to carry	verb	word	jur	law
dict	to speak	vers	to turn	manu	hand
oper	work	vis	to see	script, scrib	to write
vol, volv	to roll	vol	to wish, will	af	before
trans	across				

1. The sounds of the musicians were barely *audible* since they were standing in a soundproof room.

    ____

2. It was difficult to understand everything she was saying since she talked so much and was so *verbose*.

    ____

3. To insure his *transfer* to another division in the company, the employee told everyone he would be happy to leave.

    ____

4. The message couldn't be read because the three-year-old had *scribbled* all over the paper.

    ____

5. If it hadn't been for the *benevolent* stranger, the elderly lady would have been run over by the speeding car.

    ____

6. The students *affixed* the posters to buildings all around the campus so everyone knew about the debate.

    ____

Name _______________________________   **Date** _______________

THE BICYCLE/GHOSTS AND SHADOWS

Similes can be found in the selection "Ghosts and Shadows." A *simile* is a comparison between things that are unlike each other. The comparison is made using the word *like* or *as*. Read the quotations below, then tell what is being compared.

1. The stars peep behind her and peer:
    And I laugh to see them whirl and flee,
    Like a swarm of golden bees.

    ________________ are compared to ________________

2. The wrinkled sea beneath the eagle crawls:
    He watches from his mountain walls,
    And like a thunderbolt he falls.

    ________________ is compared to ________________

3. Silently, like thoughts come and go,
    the snowflakes fall, each one a gem.

    ________________ are compared to ________________ and ________________

4. The wind moans like a long wail from some despairing soul shut out
    in the awful storm.

    ________________ is compared to a ________________

5. Dry leaves upon the wall, which flap like rustling wings and seek
    escape.

    ________________ are compared to ________________

6. False friends are like our shadows, keeping close to us while we walk
    in sunshine, but leaving us the instant we cross into the shade.

    ________________ are compared to ________________

7. Like a river, swift and clear,
    Flows his song through many a heart.

    ________________ is compared to ________________

8. Let your life be like a snowflake, which leaves a mark but not a stain.

    ________________ is compared to ________________

9. True friendship is like sound health, the value of it is seldom known
    until it is lost.

    ________________ is compared to ________________

A Promise Kept/A Promise Broken

A. Match the parts of the following sentences to make complete sentences that tell the plot of "A Promise Kept." Draw a line to connect parts that belong together. Then number the sentences 1–8 as they happened in the story. The first one is done for you.

A.

B.

_1_ Akana, to please his adopted brother,

tells his brother why he came late.

____ Finally, Hasabe sees Adana

return on the 9th day of the 9th month.

____ Akana tells Hasabe that a man's soul

killed himself to keep a promise.

____ The 9th day of the 9th month passes

can travel two hundred miles in a day.

____ Hasabe knew that his brother

makes a promise to return on a certain day.

____ Hasabe says that no living man

approaching just as the moon is fading.

____ Hasabe and his mother prepare for Akana's

can travel a thousand miles in a day.

____ Speaking in a whisper, Adana

and it seems Akana will not come.

B. Now write the sentences as a paragraph and retell the story. Remember to indent the first sentence.

____

____

____

____

____

____

____

____

CONTINUITY OF PARKS

Tone is the writer's attitude toward his work. The tone of "Continuity of Parks" is both mysterious and suspenseful. In the Word List below are some adjectives that can be used to describe the tone an author might use in his or her work. Before you begin the exercise, review the meanings of the words. Use a dictionary to help you, or review them with a classmate.

Word List

sarcastic	angry	sincere	serious	unsympathetic
straightforward	factual	put-on	unhappy	

A. Read each statement below. Select a word from the box above that best describes the tone of the statement. Write the word in the blank.

1. _______________ Teenagers often don't work as hard as they could.

2. _______________ He had a grim look on his face as he dejectedly walked toward the gray, bleak, unkept house.

3. _______________ Teenagers are about as industrious as a cow on a 105-degree day.

4. _______________ If your parents are going through a divorce, don't worry about what went wrong in the past; think positively and spend time with friends.

5. _______________ People spend too much money, and so we have inflation. People should stop spending so much. They should plant gardens, fish for their food, sew their own clothes, chop wood for their furnaces, and ride mules to save gas.

6. _______________ Teenagers are a pack of lazy, useless bums!

7. _______________ Any teenager should be able to pass a driver's test. The fact that you failed yours is proof that you are lazy and did not apply yourself to the task. You should be ashamed of yourself for doing as badly as you did.

8. _______________ New York City is the most populated metropolitan area in the United States.

B. Write three sentences of your own that illustrate different tones. In parentheses after each sentence, identify the tone.

1. ____

2. ____

3. ____

THE STREET/BAD DREAM/A DREAM

The *theme* of a literary work is the underlying meaning or main idea the author wants to communicate to the reader. All three poems in this section have a definite theme. Read the paragraph below. Think about its theme or the main idea as you read the sentences of the paragraph.

> The man was an ordinary guy. At least that is what Carla thought when she took a ride from him. They were in the middle of nowhere when the man pulled to the side of the road. Carla had been in similar situations before. However, never in the middle of nowhere. She wondered what to do as the man moved closer to her. She felt anxious and afraid.

A. Rewrite each sentence in the paragraph in your own words.

1. ____

2. ____

   ____

3. ____

   ____

4. ____

5. ____

   ____

6. ____

   ____

7. ____

B. From the sentences you wrote, can you guess the main idea of the paragraph? Circle the letter of the best inference.

a. Carla really likes the man.
b. The man wanted to be alone with Carla.
c. The man's car ran out of gas.
d. Don't take rides with strangers.
e. Carla is nervous.

C. Do you agree with the theme? Explain your opinion. Give examples and reasons.

____

____

Name _________________________________ Date ___________

PROVERBS FROM THE TALMUD

Homophones are words that sound alike but have different spellings and meanings. *Through* and *threw* are homophones, as are *do* and *due*. **Choose the correct homophone to complete each sentence below. Use a dictionary if necessary.**

1. After cheering for two ______________ (hours, ours), he lost his voice.

2. Don't forget to ______________ (by, buy, bye) fruit and vegetables.

3. The mosquitoes began to ______________ (team, teem) throughout the swamp.

4. Use fabric ______________ (die, dye) to brighten the pillow's color.

5. Get a ______________ (bale, bail) of straw to spread in the garden.

6. A collie dog has a ______________ (rough, ruff) of fur around its neck.

7. A whole is the ______________ (sum, some) of all its parts.

8. We climbed all day to reach the ______________ (peek, peak).

9. She ______________ (one, won) two gold medals at the Olympics.

10. They may never discover ______________ (whose, who's) footprints made the track in the snow.

11. My voice was so ______________ (hoarse, horse) that I croaked like a frog.

12. A time machine might bring a visitor from the ______________ (passed, past) or the future.

13. ______________ (We'll, Wheel) just see about that!

14. He couldn't tell ______________ (which, witch) of the twins was coming toward him.

15. It is not always easy to find the ______________ (mane, main) idea of a paragraph.

PROVERBS FROM THE TALMUD

Because homophones sound alike but are spelled differently, they sometimes cause spelling problems. Read the sentences below, each of which has one or two incorrect homophones. Circle the word or words that are spelled incorrectly and then write on the line below the correct homophone for each word. You may use a dictionary if you need help.

1. The friends will go to a tropical island for a weak.

   ____

2. The whether is almost guaranteed too be hot and sunny.

   ____

3. From the ocean liner they will view the colorful sales of many small boats.

   ____

4. They will be on the see four many days.

   ____

5. If it storms, the waves may become high and ruff.

   ____

6. The passengers will have two stay below deck until the son comes out.

   ____

7. A knew and brighter day will soon begin.

   ____

8. The ocean will again bee smooth and calm.

   ____

9. Soon the beautiful islands will be in site.

   ____

10. That very knight the friends will enjoy an island feast.

   ____

An Easy Decision/Your Poem, Man …

An **antonym** is a word that has the opposite meaning from another word. For example, the antonyms *least* and *most* are contained in the work "Your Poem, Man … "

A. Circle the best antonym for each of the words in the first column. Use a dictionary if necessary.

1. buy:	purchase	sell	trade	service
2. frequent:	harsh	often	seldom	shove
3. handsome:	ugly	huge	graceful	champion
4. mammoth:	total	large	tiny	lovely
5. victory:	pain	joy	tough	defeat
6. large:	huge	small	great	bony

B. Circle the two words that are antonyms in the following sentences.

1. The clumsy girl became a graceful ballerina.

2. It's difficult to believe that such a strict teacher could be such a lenient parent.

3. After being in the water for so long the swimmers' smooth skin had become rough and dry.

4. The marriage vows state that husband and wife will be loyal in sickness and in health.

C. On the line provided, write an antonym for each underlined word.

1. The mistake he made was very serious. _______________________

2. The guard on duty was vigilant and reliable. _______________________

3. It was his misfortune to miss the train. _______________________

D. Write two sentences of your own that contain antonyms. Underline the antonyms in both sentences.

1. ____

2. ____

AN EASY DECISION/YOUR POEM, MAN …

The poems "An Easy Decision" and "Your Poem, Man … " are both filled with imagery. *Imagery* is the writer's use of words that appeal to the senses. Look at the pictures below. Then in the space provided, describe the sensory details you get from looking at and thinking about each picture. After you have done that, use the space provided to write sentences that use imagery and the sensory details you described.

1. Describe what you

see ____

____

hear ____

smell ____

Sentence: ____

____

____

2. Describe what you

see ____

____

feel ____

Sentence: ____

____

____

3. Describe what you

see ____

smell ____

taste ____

Sentence: ____

____

____

UNFOLDING BUD

Below are six hyphenated compound words. Before you look them up in a dictionary, use the space provided to write down what you think the words mean. Then use a dictionary to look up each meaning and write a sentence using the hyphenated compound word. Were you on the right track?

1. frame-up _______________________

____

____

2. heart-to-heart _______________________

____

____

3. light-handed _______________________

____

____

4. bread-and-butter _______________________

____

____

5. jack-of-all-trades _______________________

____

____

6. brother-in-law _______________________

____

____

UNFOLDING BUD

A **metaphor** is an implied comparison between two unlike things. Metaphors do not use words such as *like* or *as,* however. The poet who wrote "Unfolding Bud" compares a poem to a flower.

A. Read the sentences below and underline the part that is a metaphor. Tell what is being compared and then, in your own words, tell what the metaphor means. The first one is completed as an example.

1. Mrs. Martin trusted the lawyer until she realized he was a wolf in sheep's clothing.

   comparison: _lawyer to a wolf_________________________________

   meaning: _The lawyer was a dangerous man.___________________

2. Charles sure is a chicken-hearted guy. He won't try anything new on skis.

   comparison: ____

   meaning: ____

3. Jimmy likes to monkey around with automobile engines.

   comparison: ____

   meaning: ____

4. The donkey I was given to ride down the steep trail of the Grand Canyon moved at a snail's pace.

   comparison: ____

   meaning: ____

5. After going two days without food, the hikers wolfed down the lunch that the rescue party had prepared.

   comparison: ____

   meaning: ____

B. Write a metaphor of your own to describe each scene below.

   the sound of a kindergarten classroom
   looking at cars from the top of the Empire State building

1. ____

2. ____

   ____

BEWARE: DO NOT READ THIS POEM/ HOW TO EAT A POEM

Choose the pair of words that best completes each of the following sentences. Use context clues to help you. Circle the correct answer. The first one is completed as an example.

1. The old woman in "Beware: Do Not Read This Poem" _______________ into a _______________.

   a. ran … closet
   (c.) disappeared … mirror
   b. fell … bathtub
   d. jumped … swimming pool

2. The _______________ in the poem is _______________ .

   a. old woman … frightened
   c. tenant … indoors
   b. villagers … jealous
   d. mirror … greedy

3. More than 75 years ago, Thomas Edison _______________ the electric lightbulb, and so the popularity of kerosene lamps and _______________ decreased.

   a. imagined … reading
   c. improved … electricity
   b. invented … candles
   d. destroyed … burning

4. The barter system works on the theory of trading goods and services. Therefore, people who _______________ have little need for _______________ .

   a. buy … wealth
   c. travel … trading
   b. work … play
   d. trade … money

5. Violent crime on TV has many people upset. They feel that it influences young people to _______________ violence as a means of _______________ problems.

   a. reject … getting
   c. accept … solving
   b. get … making
   d. acquire … causing

6. A lot has changed since the Industrial Revolution. Years ago the government didn't _______________ with businesses, so no one watched to see that factory workers were treated _______________ .

   a. combine … with doctors
   c. interfere … fairly
   b. reach … disrespectfully
   d. qualify … poorly

THE TIGER

Words in the English language come from many languages. The history of a word is called its *etymology*. Review the section of your dictionary that explains the use of abbreviations and symbols. Then, look up the following words and tell the etymology of each one. Read carefully to get as much history about the word as you can. The first one is completed for you as an example.

1. husband Originally Old Norse husbondi meaning horse trader; it developed into

the Old English husbonda which became husbonde in Middle English.

Today in English the word is husband.

2. sarong ____

____

____

3. village ____

____

____

4. Allah ____

____

____

5. tiger ____

____

____

6. banana ____

____

____

7. helium ____

____

____

8. raccoon ____

____

____

Name _________________________________   Date _________________________

FIVE HAIKU

A. Look at the words in the chart below. Fill in the boxes next to each word as directed at the top of each column. The first one is completed for you as an example.

WORD	NUMBER OF VOWELS SEEN	NUMBER OF VOWELS HEARD	NUMBER OF SYLLABLES
preheat	3	2	2
interest			
writer			
classical			
haiku			
steam			
cheese			

B. Check the spelling of the following words in a dictionary. If the word is spelled correctly below, write *OK* in the space provided. Correct any incorrect spelling by writing the word in its correct form.

1. inheritence _________________

2. recommend _________________

3. secretery _________________

4. catagory _________________

5. seargeant _________________

6. teriffic _________________

7. describe _________________

8. receive _________________

C. Write out the pronunciation of the following words using the dictionary's symbols. If more than one pronunciation is given, write them all.

1. generosity _________________________________

2. lacquer _________________________________

3. measure _________________________________

4. theory _________________________________

UNTITLED/OCHO PERRITOS (EIGHT PUPPIES)

Homophones are words that are pronounced the same but have different spellings and meanings. Place the correct homophone from the box in each sentence.

Homophone	Meaning	Homophone	Meaning
grate	grind	to	toward
great	very much	too	also, very
		two	following one
all ready	prepared		
already	by the time	threw	tossed away
		through	by way of,
accept	receive		beyond,
except	other than		finished

1. The puppies liked _____________ whimper and whine.

2. The author of "Eight Puppies" thought it would be _____________ fun to be a puppy.

3. The autumn mountain shows _____________ the fog.

4. When I reached the house, he had _____________ gone.

5. We go to the university every day _____________ Sunday.

6. He decided to go _____________ the Holland Tunnel to get to his destination.

7. It's really _____________ bad you can't come with us to the museum.

8. The country's first president was a _____________ man.

9. The child was happy to _____________ the late birthday present.

10. Breakfast will be _____________ before you know it!

THREE UNTITLED POEMS

A **symbol** is anything that stands for or represents something else. For example, Uncle Sam is a symbol for the United States and a red cross is a symbol of first aid. Often poets use symbols in poems. The parrot in the first poem is a symbol for truth.

A. Choose four of the words below. Draw a symbol to represent each word you selected in a box below.

WEALTH   LOVE   TRUTH   PEACE   BEAUTY   DANGER   FRIENDSHIP

B. Use the lines in each box to write a sentence explaining why you chose your symbols.

THE PEN OF MY AUNT

A. In the play *The Pen of My Aunt,* Madame is a dynamic character. Look at the chart below and put an *X* next to the characteristics Madame possesses. Then, in the space to the right, write evidence from the play that supports your opinion. An example is completed for you. Work with a partner to finish the chart.

CHARACTERISTIC		EVIDENCE
clever	X	hiding the list of names in her quill pen
terrified		
brave		
skillful		
insecure		
considerate		
cautious		
patriotic		
unwary		

B. In the space below, write a character description of Madame using all or some of the adjectives you chose. Include evidence you cited to explain Madame's characteristics.

____

____

____

____

____

____

____

____

AFRICA'S PLEA/FOREFATHERS

Use an atlas, an encyclopedia, or your world geography text to identify the nations of Africa. Place the number of the nation in the correct space.

1. Ivory Coast
2. Libya
3. Kenya
4. Algeria
5. Liberia
6. Tanzania
7. Zimbabwe
8. Ghana
9. Zambia
10. Gabon
11. Morocco
12. Uganda
13. Benin
14. Guinea
15. Malawi
16. Niger
17. Rwanda
18. Mauritania
19. South Africa
20. Namibia
21. Sudan
22. Democratic Republic of the Congo
23. Mali
24. Sierra Leone
25. Senegal
26. Congo
27. Madagascar
28. Mozambique
29. Nigeria
30. Botswana
31. Togo
32. Central African Republic
33. Somalia
34. Burundi
35. Cameroon
36. Ethiopia
37. Tunisia
38. Chad
39. Angola
40. Egypt
41. Swaziland
42. Lesotho
43. Gambia
44. Equitorial Guinea
45. Guinea-Bissau
46. Eritrea
47. Djibouti

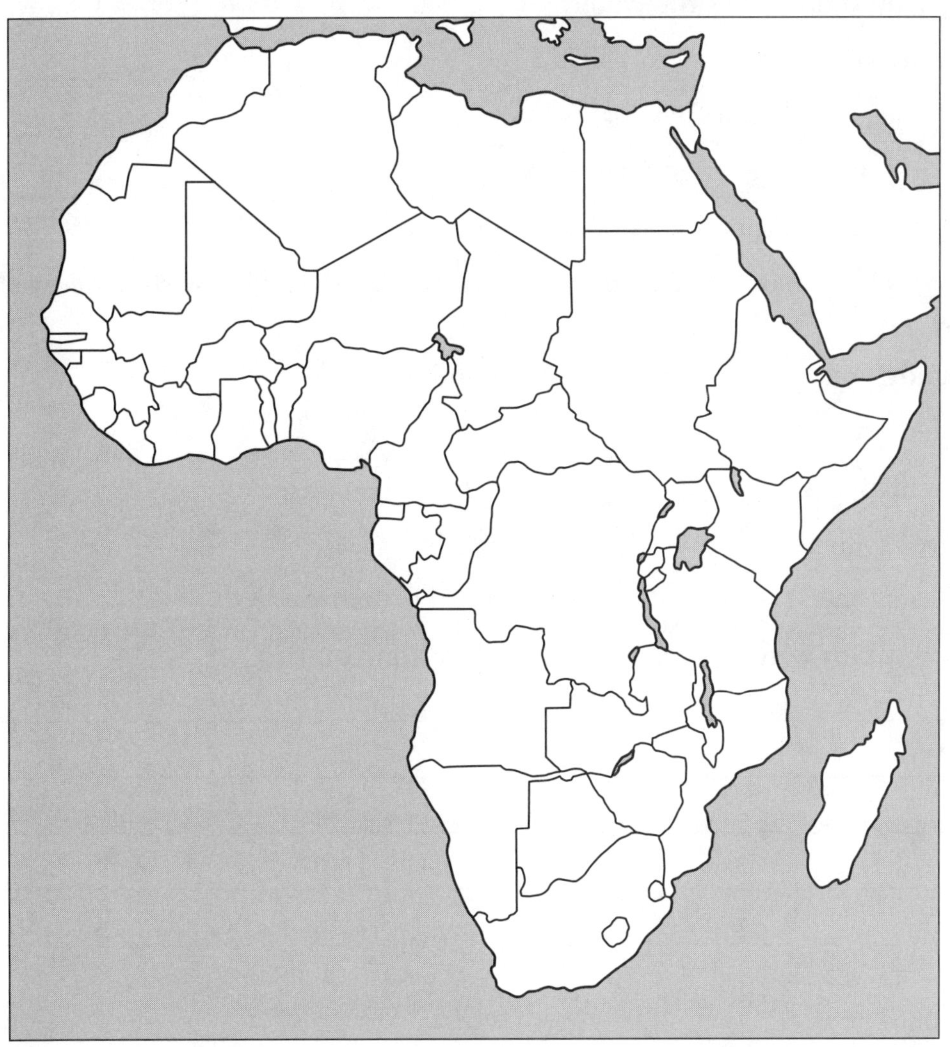

DR. HEIDEGGER'S EXPERIMENT

A. Match the name of the character from "Dr. Heidegger's Experiment" with the description given. Put the letter of the character next to the appropriate statement. Some statements will suit more than one character.

1. _____ had many suitors
2. _____ loved Sylvia Ward
3. _____ grey-bearded
4. _____ topic of scandalous stories
5. _____ once a rich merchant
6. _____ wasted his health and money
7. _____ once a politician
8. _____ would not drink the water
9. _____ decided to journey to Florida
10. _____ once very beautiful
11. _____ in love with the same woman
12. _____ kept a rose for 55 years

a. Mr. Medbourne

b. Colonel Killigrew

c. Mr. Gascoigne

d. Widow Wycherly

e. Dr. Heidegger

B. Draw a line to match the character with the quality below that he or she might symbolize.

1. Dr. Heidegger   greed
2. Mr. Medbourne   corruption
3. Colonel Killigrew   conceit
4. Widow Wycherly   dignity
5. Mr. Gascoigne   sinful pleasures

C. Briefly explain why you matched the above as you did.

____

____

____

____

EIGHTY-FIVE/LOVE SHAKES MY HEART/SHALL I?

A. The epigrams "eighty-five," "Love Shakes My Heart," and "Shall I?" were written hundreds of years ago. Below are some other expressions that have been around for a long time. Match the sayings on the left with the implied meanings on the right by supplying the correct letter. One is completed as an example.

1. __E__ People who live in glass houses shouldn't throw stones.

2. _____ Don't count your chickens before they are hatched.

3. _____ A stitch in time saves nine.

4. _____ Fine feathers make fine birds.

5. _____ Keep the home fires burning.

6. _____ Many hands make light work.

7. _____ A leopard never changes its spots.

8. _____ When the cat's away the mice will play.

9. _____ Everything comes to him who waits.

10. _____ Make hay while the sun shines.

A. The basic character of a person can't be changed.

B. Lots of people cooperating make a job easier.

C. If you are patient rather than hasty, you will get what you want.

D. Keep everything in your home, country, and so forth in good condition.

E. People with faults of their own shouldn't attack the faults of others.

F. A person can look wealthy just by wearing expensive clothes.

G. Fixing something as soon as it is needed will save a lot of time, trouble, and money.

H. Take advantage of things while you have the chance.

I. Don't expect success or victory before it happens.

J. When the person in charge is absent, others do as they like.

B. Choose two of the expressions above. Use each to write an original sentence.

1. ____

____

2. ____

____

CHRISTMAS LIGHT

A. The author of "Christmas Light" uses *personification*—giving human qualities to non-human objects—in her poem. In each of the following sentences, one part has been underlined. From the three choices given after each sentence, choose the one that uses personification to express the same meaning as the underlined part. Circle the best answer.

1. The wind isn't very strong.
   a. is barely moving the leaves on the trees
   b. gently kissed our cheeks
   c. slapped us in the face

2. My car uses a lot of gas.
   a. burns
   b. leaks
   c. guzzles

3. The waves were high because of the storm.
   a. were angry
   b. were like glass
   c. were huge

4. The mountains rise far above the clouds.
   a. are high above
   b. looked down on
   c. looked up from

5. Your car sounds like it is ready for the junk yard.
   a. going to lie down and die
   b. going to take off
   c. having mechanical problems

6. My work is very difficult for me.
   a. killing me
   b. very hard for me
   c. like a treadmill

B. Write a paragraph using personification.

____

____

____

____

Name _______________________________   *Date* _______________________

CIPHER IN THE SNOW

In the story "Cipher in the Snow," the teacher looked over Cliff Evans's file report. Unfortunately, it didn't contain much information. Pretend this is a questionnaire that will go into your school file. Fill it out so your teacher can learn more about you.

**All Around the Place School
123 Knowledge Blvd.
Anytown, USA**

Name _____________________________________ Phone _____________

Address _____________________________ City ___________ State _______

Date of birth ______________ Birthplace ____________________________

What language do you speak at home? _________________________________

Do you have any brothers or sisters? _______ What are their names and ages? _________

____

Are high grades extremely important to you? __________________________

Is it important to you to receive praise from other people? ______________

Do you or your parents emphasize your family background? Explain. ____________

____

What is your favorite holiday that you celebrate with your family? ______________

____

What are two goals you have set for yourself? _______________________

____

____

What are three qualities you look for in a friend? _____________________

____

What do you like most about yourself? _______________________________

____

____

CIPHER IN THE SNOW

Few facts were known about the student, Cliff Evans, in the story "Cipher in the Snow." The teacher, who was the narrator, had to make some conclusions about him based upon opinions. Can you tell the difference between fact and opinion?

    Key: Statements of opinion express beliefs that may or may not be true.

    Key: Statements of fact express ideas that can be proven to be true or false.

Read the sentences below. Decide whether each sentence is a statement of fact or of opinion. Write *F* in front of sentences that are facts. Write *O* in front of sentences that are opinions.

1. _____ Years ago, people were convinced that the world was flat.

2. _____ Tests are always difficult.

3. _____ Elementary school students wear uniforms in many South American countries.

4. _____ People can't be hypnotized against their will.

5. _____ People today spend too much of their spare time watching TV.

6. _____ People who are willing to work hard and do what they are told will be successful.

7. _____ The University of Southern California is in Los Angeles.

8. _____ Five percent of $100.00 is $5.00.

9. _____ The penalties for the use of illegal drugs should be stricter.

10. _____ Washington's birthday is an official holiday.

11. _____ The story was the best one in the book.

12. _____ There are some people from Japan living in Germany.

13. _____ Passenger trains are not as comfortable as they used to be.

14. _____ The black rhinoceros weighs more than a ton.

15. _____ There are "black holes" in outer space.

16. _____ Broccoli is the tastiest vegetable.

17. _____ There are fifty states in the United States.

18. _____ Summer in Maine is hotter than winter.

Name _______________________________   **Date** _______________

A LESSON IN DISCIPLINE

You learned about tone in the selection, "A Lesson in Discipline." *Tone* **is the writer's attitude about the story. Read the passages below. Circle the word or words that best describe the tone of each selection.**

1. If there's anything in the world I hate—and you know it—it is asking you for money. I'd rather go without a thing a thousand times. I'm sure, if I'd any money of my own, I'd never ask you for a cent—never! It's painful to me, gracious knows! If there is anything that humbles a poor woman, it is coming to a man's pocket for every cent. It's dreadful! (*from* "Mrs. Caudle Needs Spring Clothing," Douglas Jerrold)

   a. threatening   b. serious   c. angry   d. resentful

   What key words in the selection led you to your choice? _______________________

   ____

2. Young men you are the architects of your own fortunes. Rely upon your own strength of body and soul. Take for your star self-reliance, faith, honesty and industry. Think well of yourself. Assume your own position and rise above the envious and jealous. Fire above the mark you intend to hit. Energy and determination with a right motive are the levers that move the world … if this advice be implicitly followed by young men of the country, the millennium is at hand! (*from* "Advice to Young Men," Noah Porter)

   a. enthusiastic   b. unhappy   c. defiant   d. optimistic

   What key words in the selection led you to your choice? _______________________

   ____

3. These were the words of a blue-eyed child as she kissed her chubby hand and looked down the stairs, "Good night, papa; Jessie see you in the morning. I love you."

   It came to be a settled thing, and every evening as the mother slipped the white night-gown over the plump shoulder, the little one stopped on the stairs and sang out, "Good night papa, Jessie see you in the morning. I love you;" and as the father heard the silvery voice of the child, he came and taking the cherub in his arms, kissed her tenderly and said, "I love you, too." (anonymous)

   a. generous   b. devoted   c. pitiful   d. full of love

   What key words in the selection led you to your choice? _______________________

   ____

MELTING POT

A. *Synonyms* are words with similar meanings. For example, some synonyms for the word *melting* include *dissolving, disintegrating,* and *disappearing.* Give at least two synonyms for each of the following words, which are taken from the personal essay, "Melting Pot." Use a dictionary or a thesaurus, if necessary. The first item below is completed for you.

1. children   descendants   kin   youngsters

2. propped _____________ _____________ _____________

3. pleasant _____________ _____________ _____________

4. fable _____________ _____________ _____________

5. exactly _____________ _____________ _____________

6. moneyed _____________ _____________ _____________

7. wince _____________ _____________ _____________

8. install _____________ _____________ _____________

9. embattled _____________ _____________ _____________

10. seedy _____________ _____________ _____________

B. Using one of the synonyms you chose for each word above, write ten original sentences. Underline the word you chose to use. The first one is completed for you.

1. The <u>descendants</u> of the first settlers usually remained farmers.

2. ____

3. ____

4. ____

5. ____

6. ____

7. ____

8. ____

9. ____

10. ____

Name ____ Date _______________

RED *from* A PRECOCIOUS AUTOBIOGRAPHY

A. The story "Red" contains an introduction, body, and conclusion. Read the statements below. Put an *I* in front of any statement that could be considered part of the introduction (setting, characters, conflict). Put a *B* in front of any statement that could be considered part of the body (actions, complications), and put a *C* in front of any statement that could be considered part of the conclusion (climax, resolution).

_________________ **1.** Red beat me up with brass knuckles.

_________________ **2.** It was 1944 in Moscow.

_________________ **3.** I wrote a poem about Red.

_________________ **4.** I lived in a small apartment.

_________________ **5.** Red, a sixteen-year-old bully, ruled our street.

_________________ **6.** I felt ashamed of my cowardice and decided to do something about it.

_________________ **7.** Each time I saw Red, I ran.

_________________ **8.** I used my jujitsu on Red; he no longer ruled our street.

_________________ **9.** I learned two valuable lessons.

_________________ **10.** I practiced Japanese wrestling for three weeks.

_________________ **11.** One lesson was not to fear the strong.

B. Answer the questions below.

1. What lesson did the narrator of "Red" learn besides the one mentioned above?

____

____

____

2. What is something that you believe in that you would stand up and fight for?

____

____

____

____

MY FATHER AND THE HIPPOPOTAMUS

The selection "My Father and the Hippopotamus" is set in South Africa, on a farm about thirty miles from the Kruger National Park. Use an encyclopedia, an atlas, or your world geography text to locate and identify the following on the map of South Africa below. Place the number of each item in the correct space on the map.

1. Cape Town
2. Johannesburg
3. Namib Desert
4. Kruger National Park
5. Lesotho
6. Drakensberg Mountains
7. Pretoria
8. Atlantic Ocean
9. Indian Ocean
10. Swaziland
11. Olifants River
12. Kalahari Desert

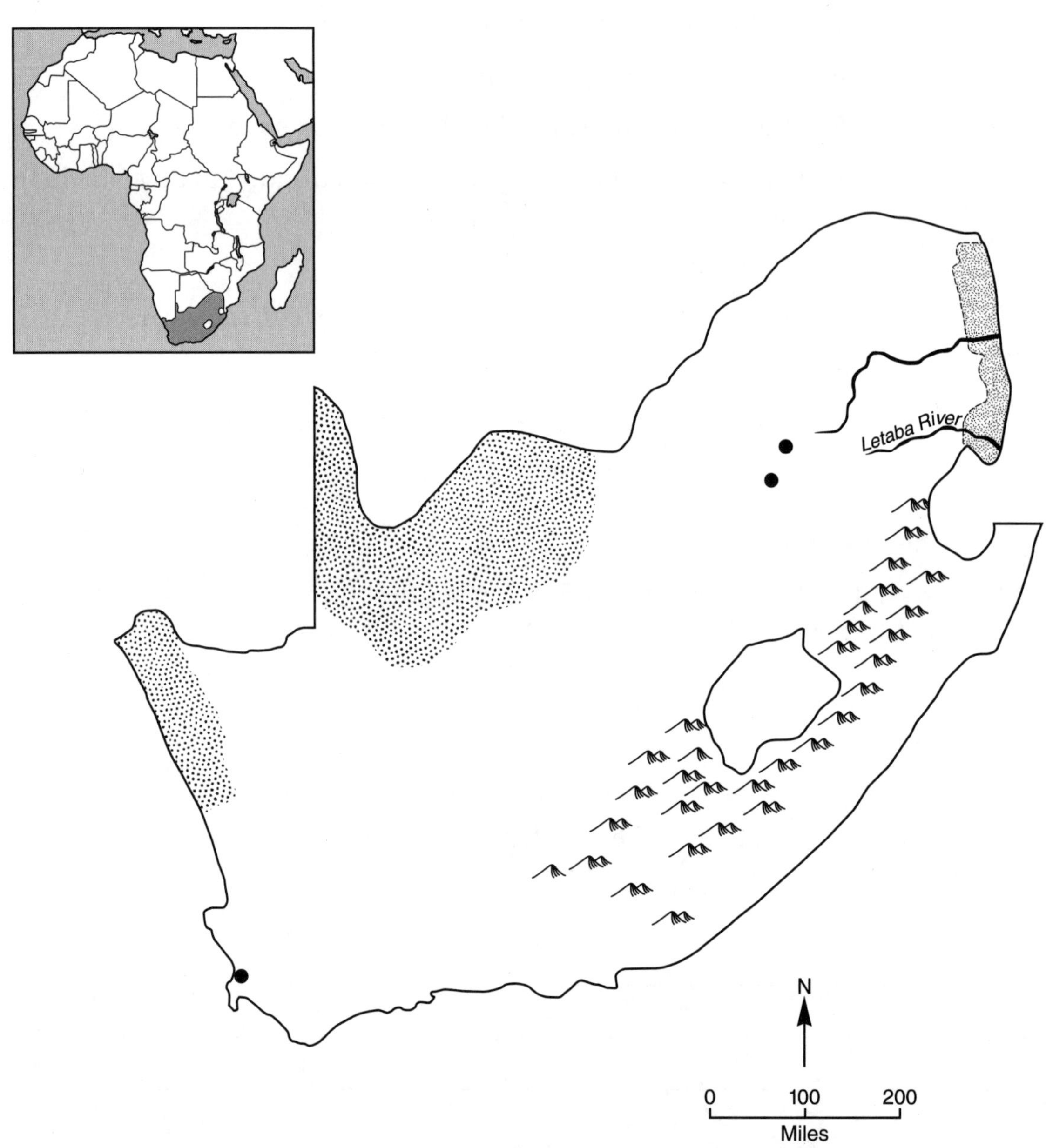

MY FATHER AND THE HIPPOPOTAMUS

Homophones are easy to confuse since they sound alike, but have different spellings and meanings. In "My Father and the Hippopotamus," you may have encountered several homophones.

In the sentences below, fill in the blank space with the appropriate word taken from the word box of homophones.

council—a meeting counsel—to advise	pain—feeling of being hurt pane—sheet of glass
tide—rise and fall of the ocean tied—past tense of *to tie*	ring—a circle wring—to twist
pair—a set of two pare—to trim off pear—fruit	assistance—aid, a helping hand assistants—people who help
team—a group of players teem—to swarm	rap—to knock, a kind of music wrap—to fold a covering around
weak—not strong week—seven days	band—group of people, narrow strip for holding things together banned—forbidden
miner—one who digs coal minor—person under 21 years of age	guessed—past tense of *to guess* guest—a visitor

1. After people complained, the heavy metal ______________ was

    ______________ from playing after eleven o'clock in the evening.

2. The pleasure boats were securely ______________ to the dock

    because an extremely high ______________ was expected.

3. Who would have ______________ that a visitor, a ______________ in
    our house, would be so thoughtless?

4. My favorite fruit is the ______________ . However, when the grocer

    packages them together in ______________s, they get bruised, and I

    have to ______________ the skin before eating them.

from KAFFIR BOY

A. Below are events from *Kaffir Boy*. Arrange the events into their proper sequence. Number them in the correct order from 1 to 8.

_______________ **1.** Problems with the boy's admittance papers and his family background are resolved.

_______________ **2.** The boy confronts his drunken father and is shunned.

_______________ **3.** The boy learns why his education is so very important to his mother.

_______________ **4.** He promises to attend school forever.

_______________ **5.** The boy learns that his father has beaten his mother.

_______________ **6.** The boy meets the principal and sees the many canes used for punishment.

_______________ **7.** The boy is given a bath and taken to school by his mother and grandmother.

_______________ **8.** With his decision, the boy's destiny is changed forever.

B. On the lines below, write a paragraph summarizing the events in the story. You may use the sentences you numbered above.

____

____

____

____

____

____

____

____

____

____

____

____

____

THE HIGHWAYMAN

Often when you don't know the meaning of a word, you ask, "How is it used?" When you do this, you are using context clues to get more ideas and information about the unfamiliar word. You may have encountered unfamiliar terms in the poem "The Highwayman."

One way to develop your skill in using context clues is to think about words that are related to certain subject matter.

A. Below you will find topics for paragraphs. List several words below each topic that you would expect to find in reading about these topics. Work with a partner and brainstorm as many as you can together.

1. Applying for a Driver's License

____

____

____

2. A Visit to the Dentist's Office

____

____

____

3. The Olympic Games

____

____

____

B. Loyalty is an important theme in "The Highwayman." Brainstorm which words in "The Highwayman" could be considered clues about loyalty.

____

____

____

MY LORD, THE BABY

The **setting** of a story is the time and place in which the action occurs. Sometimes it is nothing more than a background for the action of the story. Other times it is critical to a story because it can create and sharpen the action. The setting of "My Lord, the Baby" is in India.

A. Read the following very short story and pay close attention to the setting. Then answer the questions that follow.

As she slowly opened her eyes, she saw the shattered remains of the small airplane she had been flying. In a daze, she looked around and realized that what was left of the plane had become a part of the mountainside. She could barely recognize it as a plane at all because new fallen snow had almost completely covered it. She knew she was lucky to have survived the crash at all, but the horror of her situation came into view, and it terrified her. She was alone and way off the course she had intended to fly. She had no food, no water, no protection from the freezing elements. She knew her radio would be useless even if it were intact. As the sun sank below the snow-capped mountaintop, she heard the sound of wolves. Fighting back tears of fear and hopelessness, she said a prayer and inched toward the plane's fragmented cockpit.

1. What is the setting of the story?

____

2. What problems does the character have to deal with?

____

B. Below are different settings. How would each one change the action of the story above? List some of the problems that the settings would create for the downed pilot.

1. The desert in July at high noon

____

____

2. The ocean 100 miles from land at night

____

____

3. The African jungle during monsoon season

____

____

THE BLIND MEN AND THE ELEPHANT

Think about observations of the blind men in "The Blind Men and the Elephant." Fill in the blanks in the statements below. The first one is completed for you as an example.

1. The first man _____fell_____ against the elephant's _____side_____
    (rhymes with *well*)   (rhymes with *glide*)

    and said the elephant was like a _____wall_____ .
    (rhymes with *ball*)

2. The second man _______________ the elephant's round, smooth, sharp
    (rhymes with *melt*)

    _______________ and said the elephant was like a _______________ .
    (rhymes with *brusk*)   (rhymes with *clear*)

3. The third man _______________ the elephant's squirming
    (rhymes with *book*)

    _______________ and said the elephant was like a _______________ .
    (rhymes with *sunk*)   (rhymes with *rake*)

4. The fourth man _______________ and felt the elephant's rough
    (rhymes with *preached*)

    _______________ and said the elephant was like a _______________ .
    (rhymes with *glee*)   (rhymes with *see*)

5. The fifth man happened to _______________ the elephant's waving
    (rhymes with *much*)

    _______________ and said the elephant was like a _______________ .
    (rhymes with *dear*)   (rhymes with *man*)

6. The sixth man _______________ the elephant's swinging
    (rhymes with *pleased*)

    _______________ and said the elephant was like a _______________ .
    (rhymes with *mail*)   (rhymes with *hope*)

CAT

Below are the stanzas of "Cat" with an extra line added. Beside the line are some words that rhyme with the last word of the stanza. Try your hand at rhyming. Using one of the suggested words, or one of your own, write an additional line. Your line should continue the theme of the poem. The first stanza is completed as an example.

"CAT"

The black cat yawns,
Opens her jaws,
Stretches her legs,
And shows her claws.

My, but she has lovely paws! ______________________ (straws, laws, paws)

Then she gets up
and stands on four
Long stiff legs
And yawns some more.

______________________________________ (store, implore, galore)

She shows her sharp teeth,
And stretches her lip;
Her slice of a tongue
Turns up at the tip.

______________________________________ (clip, slip, lip, dip)

Lifting herself
On her delicate toes,
She arches her back
As high as it goes,

______________________________________ (knows, shows, grows)

She lets herself down
With particular care,
And pads away
With her tail in the air.

______________________________________ (care, dare, hair, swear)

Work with a partner and take turns reading your poems with their new lines. Do you like how the poem sounds with your new lines? Decide if an additional line to each stanza changed the feeling of the poem. Talk about this with your partner.

CONCRETE MIXERS

"Concrete Mixers" contains examples of alliteration and onomatopoeia. **Alliteration** and **onomatopoeia** are devices used by poets to emphasize words.

KEY: *Alliteration* is the repeating of initial consonant sounds.
EXAMPLE: A tale of terror told their terrible toils of treachery.

KEY: *Onomatopoeia* is the use of words that echo the action or sound associated with a word.
EXAMPLE: tinkle, whisper, buzzing

A. Select a word from the Word List that describes the sound or the action of each of the following.

Word List

splash	crunch	whisper	clang
crash	whirl	boom	buzz
hiss	squeak	sizzle	zoom
squeal	ding-dong	whizzing	tinkle

1. ________________   bacon frying in a hot iron skillet
2. ________________   eating popcorn
3. ________________   bees swarming around their hive
4. ________________   a helicopter flying above
5. ________________   old, rusty hinges on an opening door
6. ________________   a person jumping into a swimming pool
7. ________________   wind chimes in a gentle breeze
8. ________________   a tire losing air
9. ________________   a drum in a parade

B. Choose some of the following words and write two sentences that use alliteration.

below, balloon, baby, bounced, burst, bubble, bright, bring, babble, ball

____

____

CONCRETE POETRY

The words in a concrete poem are arranged in a shape that helps communicate the main idea of the poem. Some concrete poems can be very simple—they use only a few words. The poem about the apple and the one about silence are good examples. Other concrete poems can have more complicated sentences. Either way the shape of the poem contributes to its meaning.

Work with a partner and write your own concrete poem.

1. Before you begin, brainstorm about possible subjects for your poem. Think about animals, feelings, or objects that have some importance to you. For example, you might choose to write about love in the shape of a heart. Jot down your ideas on the lines below.

   ____

   ____

   ____

2. Which idea do you and your partner like the best? Write your subject here.

   ____

   ____

3. Now, freewrite the words and phrases you will use in your concrete poem.

   ____

   ____

   ____

   ____

4. Finally, draw the shape for your poem and fill in the words in the space below. If you wish, do a final copy on another piece of paper.

AFTER YOU, MY DEAR ALPHONSE

A. Match each action and statement with the character it suits in the selection "After You, My Dear Alphonse." Write the letter of the character next to the appropriate statement. More than one letter may fit an action or statement.

A. Mrs. Wilson

B. Johnny

C. Boyd

1. _____ didn't like stewed tomatoes

2. _____ had a father who was a factory foreman

3. _____ was *very* polite

4. _____ has preconceived ideas about black people

5. _____ brought a friend home for lunch

6. _____ said, "After you, my dear Alphonse."

7. _____ offered to give old clothes

8. _____ liked to play soldier

9. _____ were mother and son

10. _____ were good friends

11. _____ made wrong assumption about a factory job

12. _____ treated each other fairly

13. _____ took gingerbread off the table

14. _____ had a father who was short

15. _____ was surprised that the sister would be a teacher

B. One theme of the story could be that prejudice and preconceived ideas are hard to hide. Circle the statements or actions above that illustrate this theme.

C. List three statements made by Johnny's mother that reveal her preconceived ideas about Boyd.

EXAMPLE: "You shouldn't let Johnny make you carry all that wood."

1. ____

2. ____

3. ____

from INVISIBLE MAN/THE INVISIBLE WOMAN

Both "Invisible Man" and "The Invisible Woman" contain many words that have special connotations: such as *flesh, possess, sideshows.* **Connotation** is the image, emotion, or association brought up by a certain word. Words may have different connotations for different people. **Denotation** is simply the literal dictionary definition of a word.

Pronounce each of the following words. First, decide if your reaction is pleasant or unpleasant. Then, write down three words that come to your mind. This will help you understand what is meant by connotation. Next, write the dictionary meaning of the word. The first one is completed as an example.

1. mother

    _____ love _____   _____ devotion _____   _____ warmth _____

    a woman as she is related to her child or children; a woman who has borne

    a child

2. snake

    _______________   _______________   _______________

    ____

    ____

3. Sunday

    _______________   _______________   _______________

    ____

    ____

4. smoke

    _______________   _______________   _______________

    ____

    ____

5. dog

    _______________   _______________   _______________

    ____

    ____

Name ____ *Date* _______________

POINT OF VIEW

"Point of View" is rich in **adverbs**—words that tell *how, where, when,* or *to what degree.* Most adverbs end in *-ly.* However, many common adverbs do not, such as *here, always, never, soon,* and *too.* In addition, some adjectives may end in *-ly* (a *likely* story, an *only* child, the *early* train). To avoid confusion, remember the following facts.

ADVERBS modify a verb, adjective, or another adverb.

(v.) Come *close.* (adverb *close* modifies verb *come*)
(adj.) It was a *very* cold day. (adverb *very* modifies adjective *cold*)
(adv.) She came *very near.* (adverb *very* modifies adverb *near*)

ADJECTIVES modify nouns.

That was a *close* decision. (adjective *close* modifies noun *decision)*
It was a *cold* day. (adjective *cold* modifies noun *day)*
That was a *near* escape. (adjective *near* modifies noun *escape)*

A. Read each sentence below. If the underlined word is an adverb, circle it. If it is an adjective, draw a box around it.

1. That is a likely story, Bob, but were you there?

2. You look well. You slept well last night, and this morning you ate a hearty meal.

3. The clouds are drifting very low today.

4. The magician opened the box somewhat cautiously.

5. It was a generous and friendly gesture.

6. Lately there have been several attempts to float the ship again.

7. Throw it high in the air.

8. He played the guitar surprisingly well.

9. The early worm gets a fair reward for getting up early.

B. Write a brief story in which each sentence contains both the adjective and the adverb form of the same word. Your story may be humorous and even nonsensical. Have fun!

Example: The awful noise upset me awfully.

____

____

____

SOUTHBOUND ON THE FREEWAY

Homophones are often misused because they sound alike. "Southbound on the Freeway" contains a number of homophones: through/threw, see/sea, red/read. Homophones are spelled differently and have different meanings, so it is important to know which one to use.

In the sentences below, fill in the blank spaces with the appropriate word. If you need help, consult a dictionary.

1. berry, bury

My dog, Claudius, likes to _____________ his bone in a special place.
Grandmother said that eating only one _____________ was not easy.

2. blue, blew

Nancy _____________ the candles out.
He wore a _____________ shirt.

3. find, fined

It's hard to _____________ your way in a storm.
Roger was _____________ fifty cents for not returning the book on time.

4. cellar, seller

Both the buyer and the _____________ must sign the agreement.
The attic is at the top of a house and the _____________ is at the bottom.

5. desert, dessert

Chocolate cake is a popular _____________ .
In her time of need, she was glad that her friends didn't _____________ her.

6. flee, flea

The cat was given a _____________ bath.
Women and children had to _____________ from their homes.

7. know, no

I _____________ you will do the best job that you can.
Hurry! There is _____________ time to waste.

8. your, you're

_____________ taxi is here.
_____________ not ready to leave, are you?

Name _________________________________   Date _________________

THE SPARROW

The narrator of "The Sparrow" makes many statements about what he sees. Some statements are main ideas and others are details. You can distinguish main ideas from related details. This skill will help you better understand the meaning of an entire selection.

A. In the space provided, label each of the following sentences as main idea (MI) or detail (D).

_____________ **1.** Certain substances that pollute the air have proven to be poisonous to animals.

_____________ Dogs and cats seem to suffer from smog the same way humans do.

_____________ **2.** Corn is an important grain that is grown in the United States and sold as a cereal.

_____________ Cereals that produce a grain are used for food.

_____________ **3.** One type of propaganda used in advertising is repetition.

_____________ To keep an idea in the mind of consumers, the advertiser will present it over and over again.

_____________ **4.** Dinosaurs lived during the prehistoric age known as the Mesozoic.

_____________ Tyrannosaurus Rex, Brontausaurus, and Triceratops are three prehistoric creatures that roamed the earth millions of years ago.

B. Main ideas and details move from the general to the specific. Look at the topics below. Name two more specific ideas after the first word. Name two more specific ideas after the second word and name one more specific idea after the third word. The first one is completed as an example.

1. Entertainment _______movies_______   _______television_______

Television _______comedy_______   _______drama_______

Comedy _______Bill Cosby Show_______

2. Sports _______________   _______________

Football _______________   _______________

Pro Team _______________

MIRROR

In the poem "Mirror" Sylvia Path uses a number of words that can be
broken into word parts, such as *preconceptions, darkness,* and *important.*

**A. One way to build your vocabulary is to learn word parts that are used over and
over. Below are some prefixes, suffixes, and roots. See if you can build at least three
words that use each word part. Ask a friend to collaborate. You can make it a word-
building game. The first one is completed as an example.**

ab	absent	abstain	abdicate
logy			
auto			
bi			
in			
micro			
photo			
tri			
trans			

B. *Appear* **is a root word. By adding prefixes and suffixes, you can create many words.
How many can you make from the words** *appear, import,* **and** *play***? (Hint: Try the
prefixes** *re-* **and** *dis-***; use the suffixes** *-s, -ing, -ed, -ance.***)**

C. Find the root word in the words below. Circle it. Use it in an original sentence.

1. justice ____

____

2. misinform ____

____

3. dissatisfied ____

____

BEAR/THE PUNCHING CLOCK

"Bear" and "The Punching Clock" both contain figures of speech such as similes, metaphors, and examples of personification.

A. Read the following paragraph and underline the similes, metaphors, and the examples of personification. If necessary, review the above figures of speech as explained in your literature text.

I had waited all day for this moment like a child waiting for Santa Claus. But the television is a fickle friend. It insisted that I sit through a commercial as boring as a hot dog without mustard. Then, without warning it began making faces at me. The clear, sharp picture became a blur of wavy lines that looked like a permanent wave. I pleaded with this spoiled child to behave, but it made faces worse than before. In complete frustration, I became a bully and began to pound on its head. It cried from the pain and sounded like a cat whose tail had been stepped upon. Then suddenly, without warning, it stopped and just sat there with a blank stare on its face. I felt like a soldier defeated in battle.

B. Now, write each of the lines you underlined on the space provided. Tell if it is a simile (S), metaphor (M), or an example of personification (P). The first two have been done for you.

1. __S__ like a child waiting for Santa Claus _________________________________
2. __M__ fickle friend ____
3. ____ ____
4. ____ ____
5. ____ ____
6. ____ ____
7. ____ ____
8. ____ ____
9. ____ ____
10. ____ ____
11. ____ ____
12. ____ ____

THREE LETTERS AND A FOOTNOTE

The salutation, or greeting, in the letter to the editor in the selection
"Three Letters and a Footnote" indicated that it was a business letter.
The salutation read, "Sir:". Business letters that are well written follow
generally accepted rules as to their form.

The parts of a business letter are the following: heading, inside address,
salutation or greeting, body, closing and signature.

**A. Look at the sample business letter below and identify the parts where indicated.
Use your English text as a reference, if necessary.**

_________________ **1.**   327 East Walnut Street
Glendale, California 41012

March 20, 2001

Department of English
Oregon State College   **2.** _________________
Corvallis, Oregon 38190

Dear Professor Potts: **3.** _________________

You requested that I send you a copy of my book *Metaphors in Poetry*.
Unfortunately, the book is sold out, so I will be unable to send it to you until
its next printing.   **4.** _________________
Thank you for your inquiry. I will let you know as soon as I have additional copies.

_________________ **5.**   Very truly yours,

_________________ **6.**   Miss Helen Throckmorton

**B. In the space below, use your imagination and create the missing parts of the letter
sent to the editor and the parts of the letter sent from the editor in "Three Letters and
a Footnote." Include the heading, inside address, greeting, body (just write a few
sentences), the closing, and the signature. Notice the editor's initials and the author's
name.**

THE BEAR

Most stories, novels, and plays revolve around some sort of struggle or conflict. For example, in the play *The Bear*, there is one conflict—Mrs. Popov vs. Smirnov. Most readers want to read to the end of the story to see how the conflict or conflicts will end.

There are several basic types of conflict that can be used by a writer. Some of these types include:

A.   people against people

B.   people against nature

C.   people against society

D.   people at odds with themselves

E.   people against the supernatural

Tell which type of conflict each of the examples below is. Put the correct letter next to the example.

1. _____   A man is hunted like an animal by another man.

2. _____   A boy can read people's minds and make them do whatever he wants them to do.

3. _____   A woman works to stop the use of pesticides that contaminate the nation's food supply.

4. _____   A pioneer family struggles to stay alive when a major drought causes their water supply to disappear.

5. _____   A boy takes ten dollars from a wallet he finds and then learns that the wallet belongs to his teacher. He struggles to decide whether to return the money.

6. _____   A tidal wave threatens the inhabitants of a small village on a remote island in the South Pacific.

7. _____   A student can't decide whether or not to give her best friend the answers to a history test. If she doesn't, her friend will fail. If she does, she will feel guilty.

8. _____   A man and a woman argue and fight from the first day they meet.

9. _____   A young man struggles to survive in the desert without food or water.

THE BEAR

The author of *The Bear*, Anton Chekhov, was a master at using words. He definitely knew the difference between **connotation** and **denotation** because he always seemed to say things in the most pleasing way.

A. Look at the words below. Draw a line matching words of similar meaning. Then circle all the words that have a more positive connotation. Use a dictionary if you need to. An example is completed for you.

1.	difficult	exhausted
2.	fired	storyteller
3.	eager	challenging
4.	tired	frugal
5.	arrogant	impatient
6.	cheap	plain
7.	unconcerned	slender
8.	liar	proud
9.	inquire	easygoing
10.	skinny	interrogate
11.	ugly	discharged

B. Choose four pairs of the words above and use them in sentences to show their differences; for example, "The teacher said the test was challenging. The students said it was difficult."

1. ____

2. ____

3. ____

4. ____

from THE TRAGEDY OF JULIUS CAESAR

In Shakespeare's play *The Tragedy of Julius Caesar*, some of the characters don't gather enough facts and ideas before they draw a conclusion. This causes trouble and chaos.

Drawing a conclusion is simply a matter of putting facts together and adding what you already know about life. It is an important skill.

Read each item below and draw a conclusion based on what you read. Circle the best answer.

1. Julius Caesar heard two interpretations of his dream. His wife told him to stay home because she feared he was in great danger. The conspirators told him the dream showed how great a man he was. Julius Caesar accepted the conspirators' interpretation.

   Julius Caesar must have been a little bit
      a. vain   b. foolish   c. pleased

2. The man climbed carefully under the weight of his supplies. With every step he took, more pebbles fell down to the ground below.

   The man is
      a. at the beach   b. on a mountainside   c. climbing a tree

3. The raccoons had invaded the campground during the night and had eaten all the food the campers had left on the picnic table. Now, they were curled up and lay fast asleep in the back of the pickup.

   The raccoons now feel
      a. contented   b. hungry   c. playful

4. The sky looks very dark and there are huge grey clouds overhead. Yesterday, the news predicted stormy weather and lots of moisture.

   There is probably going to be
      a. a blizzard   b. rainy weather   c. a tornado

5. Whenever Jasper eats spicy food, he gets an upset stomach and heartburn. Today, for lunch, he ate Mexican food with lots of chili peppers.

   Jasper feels
      a. full   b. sick   c. satisfied

from THE TRAGEDY OF JULIUS CAESAR

William Shakespeare, the poet and dramatist, lived from 1564–1616. He wrote his plays in what we know as Early Modern English. Some words that Shakespeare used are no longer considered modern. They have ceased to be in use or they have changed their meanings. Dictionaries identify these words by writing *archaic* next to their definition.

Look up the following words in a dictionary. Remember to find the word *archaic* and then give the original meaning on the line provided. Next, give the present-day definition. One is completed for you as an example.

1. tire

   archaic definition   to attire or dress _______________________________

   modern definition   to be in need of rest _______________________________

2. brave

   archaic definition   _______________________________

   modern definition   _______________________________

3. cheapen

   archaic definition   _______________________________

   modern definition   _______________________________

4. couch

   archaic definition   _______________________________

   modern definition   _______________________________

5. art

   archaic definition   _______________________________

   modern definition   _______________________________

6. mantle

   archaic definition   _______________________________

   modern definition   _______________________________

ANNE FRANK: THE DIARY OF A YOUNG GIRL

Adjectives and adverbs are modifying words that add detail to nouns and verbs. They not only expand a sentence, but they make it more interesting and meaningful.

> KEY: ADJECTIVES are words that describe or modify nouns or pronouns.
> EXAMPLE: *strong* coffee
> *happy* child
> *foolish* decision

> KEY: ADVERBS are words that describe the action of verbs and modify adjectives, other adverbs and whole groups of words.
> EXAMPLE: *extremely* happy
> *very* quickly
> drove *almost* to the end

The sentences below are very basic and uninteresting. Add some adjectives and adverbs before or after the underlined words to help these sentences come alive. An example is completed for you.

1. Anne Frank and her family hid in an attic.

____

2. She wrote in her journal.
She diligently wrote in her private journal. _______________

3. Life was hard during World War II.

____

4. The building looked old.

____

5. The water sounds loud in the morning.

____

6. People used the building for work.

____

7. He ate the bread.

____

8. Rain fell.

____

ANNE FRANK: THE DIARY OF A YOUNG GIRL

It would be difficult to read Anne Frank's diary and feel that you didn't know her. Since she wrote about her thoughts and actions, you are able to be part of them.

Select one of the three words or phrases that best completes the sentence about Anne Frank and her experiences. Circle the letter of the word or phrase and then write it in the blank.

1. Anne decided to write a diary because she didn't have a _____________ friend.

    a. sincere   b. real   c. boy

2. The suffering of Anne and her family really began when the _____________ arrived.

    a. Germans   b. grandmother   c. Russians

3. When Anne's father was sent a "call-up" notice, Anne pictured _____________ .

    a. moving to Holland   b. a phone   c. concentration camps

4. Anne packed her _____________ first when she had to go into hiding.

    a. diary   b. old letters   c. school books

5. The only goodbye Anne said was to her _____________ Moortje.

    a. next door neighbor   b. dog   c. cat

6. Anne talked about buying new clothes after the war, but said they should save every penny to _____________ .

    a. move to America   b. help other   c. buy a new house
                               people

7. Anne felt _____________ when she talked about the war because of all the misery it caused.

    a. pity and shame   b. elated   c. sad and gloomy

8. Anne's ambition was to become a(n) _____________ .

    a. wife and mother   b. artist   c. journalist

9. Anne felt it was much _____________ to be an adult than a child.

    a. more difficult   b. easier   c. more fair

10. A belief that Anne held was that people are basically _____________ .

    a. good   b. foolish   c. opinionated

MARRIAGE IS A PRIVATE AFFAIR

As you read "Marriage Is a Private Affair," you are likely to come across words that are unfamiliar to you. **Context clues** can help you determine the meaning of an unfamiliar word. When you come across a word you don't know, look for hints in the sentence to help you infer a word's meaning. Check to see whether there is one of the following:

- a hidden definition
- a carefully placed synonym
- a description of the action of the word

A. Read each of the following sentences carefully; circle the letter of the best answer.

1. Sometimes clouds will float all alone in the sky; at other times, they seem to group closely together and form *tufts.*

    A *tuft* is   a. part of a cloud.   b. some grass.   c. pictures.   d. a cluster.

2. Wearing a wedding ring is not necessary when you are married; however, it has become an *essential* part of the marriage tradition.

    Essential means   a. a basic part.   b. a traditional part.   c. expensive.   d. an extra.

3. Habits are behaviors that someone learns because of doing something over and over again. The *repetition* of the behavior turns it into a habit.

    Repetition means   a. making time for something.   b. avoiding things.
    c. doing something again and again.   d. keeping away.

4. The *teeter-totter,* which went from high to low, delighted the children, and they laughed and giggled whenever it was their turn to play.

    A *teeter-totter* is   a. a saw.   b. a ride that goes around.   c. a ride that goes side to side.   d. a ride that goes up and down.

5. Millions of Americans find themselves overeating. For this reason, *obesity* has become a real cause of concern in this country.

    Obesity means   a. the state of being overweight.   b. dinner.
    c. drinking beverages.   d. chewing food.

6. Carolyn could speak several languages easily. She was *fluent* in English, Spanish, and French.

    Fluent means   a. stammering.   b. able to speak or write with smoothness.
    c. clumsy.   d. international.

B. After you have completed the above exercise, consult a dictionary to be sure your choices were correct. For any incorrect choices you made, write sentences of your own, using the word or words in the proper context.

ALONE/EMPTY

Poets often use **figurative language**. This is language that has a meaning other than the usual meaning of the words.

The sentences below include words that have a figurative meaning. Select from the list below the clear meaning of the underlined words. Write the letter of the correct answer in the space provided. The first one is completed as an example.

A. raining very hard

B. write me a letter

C. received loud applause from the audience

D. leave him alone

E. had a strong positive effect on me

F. a talent for growing plants

G. trying to trick me

H. told the secret by accident

1. __E__ Hearing Maya Angelou read really knocked me out last night; she was great!

2. ____ I already knew about the party because Sara let the cat out of the bag.

3. ____ Carl Sagan got a big hand when he talked about the possibility of life in outer space.

4. ____ My fifteen-year-old brother is always telling me to get lost.

5. ____ It's raining cats and dogs, which really surprises me since it was so sunny this morning.

6. ____ Because she has a green thumb, I always ask her to water my plants when I go on vacation.

7. ____ I think you must be pulling my leg about the lottery ticket.

8. ____ When you get settled in your new home, please drop a line and let me know how you like it.

If Not Higher

Each exercise below contains three parts of one thought. Order and number the parts 1, 2, 3, and then write the sentence with the correct capitalization and punctuation. One is completed as an example.

1. __2__ gets up every Friday

   __3__ and he disappears

   __1__ the Rabbi of Nemerov

   The Rabbi of Nemerov gets up every Friday, and he disappears. __________

2. ____ the people decide

   ____ one day a week

   ____ the rabbi goes to heaven

   ____

3. ____ Moses can't even get there

   ____ the Lithuanian laughs

   ____ when he says that

   ____

4. ____ hides in the rabbi's room

   ____ the Lithuanian

   ____ in the evening

   ____

5. ____ before he goes out

   ____ the rabbi gets up

   ____ and dresses as a peasant

   ____

6. ____ the rabbi chops down the tree

   ____ splits it into small logs

   ____ and ties a cord around the bundle

   ____